Ministering Thoughts

*Poetry to speak to your heart, inspire your mind,
and minister to your soul*

TULSA

ISBN: 978-1-957262-37-6
Ministering Thoughts

Yorkshire Publishing
1425 E 41st Pl
Tulsa, OK 74105
www.YorkshirePublishing.com
918.394.2665

Published in the USA

Ministering Thoughts

*Poetry to speak to your heart, inspire your mind,
and minister to your soul*

By

Lady LaToya Richburg

"Set Your MINDS on things above, not on earthly things."
Colossians 3:2 NIV

Contents

Dedications

Michael L. Richburg

When God spoke the Word through his servant telling me, "I am going to show you the beauty of marriage," never did I perceive to receive a man who surpassed the desires of my heart. My mind was not ready to conceive such a notion, while my heart needed the compassion of someone strong enough to mend that which was broken. You have been with me through the ups and downs of life. I would not trade one step, not one second, nor any portion of the blessing of having you as my husband and best friend. Thank you is not enough, yet still, I would be remiss not to include it in the expression of my gratitude. I love you my husband, my lord, my king forever and always.

My Children

I have two of the greatest children a mother could ever ask for. My beautiful, intelligent daughter Ahnystie and handsome, clever son Jeremiah are a mother's dream. I love and appreciate you both. Each moment shared is beautiful to me. As you get older, my love for you continues to grow. May you continue to blossom into the great woman and man of God that you are called to be. Most certainly you two are a blessing and my gift from God!

To my Supporters

You saw the humble beginning
of a gentle soul
Eager, excited, and ready to grow
Beyond the hope of a dream,
And manifestation in the mind
You brought life to the living
For reality to find

Apostle Michael L. Richburg
Claude and Carolyn Levine
Apostle R. Frasier
Apostle Dr. P.O. Coleman
Apostle Prophet Moses Townsend Jr.
Apostle Dudley Thompson
Prophetess Eva Thompson

Thank You

Foreword

LaToya came from the name of the celebrity LaToya Jackson at the time of your birth in 1984 because you are destined for greatness. We knew your strength would not be drawn from that but from the Holy Spirit and grace of God. You are a blessing filling in the gap for your family throughout your life. We are blessed to have you. We have no favorites, just a favorite one at a time. The right thing may not always be right but continue loving God and do the best thing. We love you and are proud of you.

Mom and Dad
Claude and Carolyn Levine

Foreword

I thoroughly enjoyed your poetry!! It touched on every aspect of life. It encourages us to live an abundant life not just for ourselves, but to also be a blessing. It gives us a way to be vulnerable and strong. Excellent work!!!

This is a gem for the body of Christ.

For His Glory!!!

Job well done!!!!!!!

Pastor Jacklyn Miller

Foreword

Lady LaToya Richburg is a true woman of God that shows God's love and compassion. Lady LaToya is like a David of the Bible; she really is a woman after God's own heart. So because of that compassion and the love that she has for God and His Word that He has gracefully given us, LaToya opens up her heart and love for God's Word. In this book of Ministering Thoughts, Lady LaToya shows us in a clear and loving way just how much God loves, cares, and has compassion for us even when we don't deserve it. Lady LaToya takes us on the journey that she has with the Lord. She has allowed us on that journey so that we too can become men and women after God's own heart. So, with saying that, I encourage you to open up your hearts, minds, and spirit so that she can usher you to the place that the Lord has prepared for you. Also, please know that this book will bless you for many years to come. So, I urge you to keep it in a safe place so that you can always go back to it in order to draw nearer and nearer to our Lord and Savior. Last but not least, pass along this book title so others can grow closer to our Savior.

Minister Kimberly Wells

Part 1

Think On His LOVE

The poems in this section are written to remind you of the power of God's love. Often times we can get so overwhelmed with the different facets of our lives, until we forget one of the greatest gifts of all...Smile and bask in the warmth of His Love.

Sentimental

I desire much for you
Abundance and prosperity
Not to aimlessly wander
Without purpose, without destiny

I sustain you omnipotently
Eternal without end, right from the start
When you begin to know me
You begin to understand the sentiments of my heart

My heart feels just like you
My heart wants more, more for you

My heart hurts when you stray afar
Longing for you to know the sentiments of my heart.

For I know the thoughts that
I think towards you
I know your joys, I know your sorrows too
So when the storms come to tear you apart
Think not of your storm but on the sentiments of my heart.

Scriptures to minister to your thoughts:

Jeremiah 29:11-13

Lost and Found

I was lost, didn't know who I was
Unfulfilled, trying to fill the void in my heart
I felt undeserving, yet still I was searching for something more
Never knew, I'd find me in You

For my Hope is in you Jesus
Your joy is my strength
Your words are life to awaken my soul
It's in you that I am whole
I will praise you forevermore

Never knew, I'd find me in You

Scriptures to minister to your thoughts:

Psalm 94:17-19

First Love

Do you remember me?

I had all your time, all your attention
It was hard to speak a word,
or even think a thought
Without wanting to mention…

How great I was to you

How wonderful I made you feel
You found what you thought
was not possible
The emotional bliss seemed so surreal

So what happened?

Everything you said I was to you,
I still am
Was my prominence only in the euphoria of a moment?
Or is it that I no longer fit in the confines of
your regularly scheduled program?

So what happened?

Everything that you said I am able to do
I am still able
Was my strength based on the
circumstances of life?
Or is it that you flow with the
waves of what you see?
Back and forth, double-minded, unstable

What happened to your first love?

Scriptures to minister to your thoughts:

Revelation 2:3-5

If I...

If I could ever tell
of all the love in my heart for you,
I would speak every kind word and joyful expression,
never-ending sentiments of passionate truth

If I could ever show you
all the love that my heart feels,
We would be on an endless journey with infinite
moments of immeasurable care and zeal

If I could ever give you
all the love that my heart holds,
The streams, the rivers, and the oceans would have no
separation and give up every hidden treasure untold

Scriptures to minister to your thoughts:

Jeremiah 31:3   **John 3:16**

Dedicated to Apostle and Pastor Frasier of Love Chapel Deliverance Inc. along with all the ministry affiliates spreading the Gospel and love of Jesus Christ.

His Love

I messed up, I know I did
Just like Adam and Eve, I hid
I felt the guilt, I felt the shame
When I finally mustered up enough courage, I came
To you Jesus, And you said, "I love you"

Yes I know, it happened
I did it again
I wanted to and didn't want to
It's a war within
Now surely I am not worthy
of your mercy and grace,
Yet still I find myself yearning
for your embrace
And you say, "I love you"

Now I am certain
This surely must be it
I tried and tried but can't seem to quit
So why even bother?
What's the purpose of it all?
And you say, "I love you, answer my call"
Come with your burdens,
your issues, your past
Come with your baggage,
to me your cares you should cast

Come believing that I am
Come believing that I can
I will help your unbelief

Place your hope in my plan

For I so love you, I gave
I so love you, I died
I so love you, I rose
And gave you abundant life

I so love you, I didn't leave you comfortless
I give you pastors after my own heart
I so love you, I made you joint heirs
As a new creature, you have a new start
Look not at your condition
Look not at your sin
See the hope set before you
Keep choosing life to begin

Life, over death
Life, over what held you back
Life, over bad decisions
That led you to the wrong track
Heed not to aimless words
Nor take consolation in your
works and deeds
I am here, I love you
Make the choice to keep choosing me

Scriptures to minister to your thoughts:

John 21:15-19   **Jeremiah 3:14-15**

Romans 7:21-25

Part 2

Think On His HOPE

For some, Hope may seem like a waste of time, somewhat similar to a wishing well. Maybe it will happen, and then maybe it won't. However, for me, Hope is a path to Faith that does not rely on a two-sided coin. The focus or concern is not chances of "if" things will happen. You do not wait anxiously only to experience defeat. You find joy in knowing that the God we serve is able to make it happen for you, even if it does not happen when you think it should. Your Hope is not misplaced, even when you feel displaced. He is still God.

Here

──────

How did I get here?
Permeated in the emotionalism of my circumstances,
Taking glances
At every image that passes me
Being tugged into a whirlwind,
I see but I can't see

Why am I here?
The road I traveled
seemed to be clear in sight
Mountain highs and valley lows,
But that's normal on the journey, right?

Should I be here?
To know what I know
and having seen what I've seen
Words prophetically spoken from the beginning to end,
Yet I'm floating through the "in-between"

HERE
a place we too often find ourselves
Frustrated with what is,
hoping for what can be,
Yet frequented by glimpses of what was

HERE

Scriptures to minister to your thoughts:

James 1:2-8

Empty

Empty me – Lord fill me up again
Unshackle me – from bondage of this world
and wars within

Let your Word be a lamp unto my feet
Lord your yoke, not my will
Without you, I am blind and cannot see
Empty me – fill me up again

See…many cry, "Fill me up God, let my cup overflow,"
But to be filled, you must first be empty
For when God pours out,
what room is there for Him to grow?

Inside of you – inside of me
A filled cup feels the effects of the overflow, you see

There is no change
to the substance that is harbored within
It profits nothing to take old wine
and put it in new wineskin

Nor can we take the new
and place it into old shadows of the past
A new identity, but the identity is masked

So what is cannot be seen and what was is in-between
Hindering a transformation on the inside,
Only changing an appearance to the eyes

And we become lost, trying to be free - The change
never comes if you cannot be empty

Scriptures to minister to your thoughts:

Matthew 16:24-26

Dear Lord actually came to me as a song. Someone dear to me was going through a rough time. I really had no words to help. As they were going through, I heard these words ringing in my ear. This poem is dedicated to them and everyone who goes through those rough patches in life, when you feel like you are doing all you know how to do. Be blessed.

Dear Lord

When I've prayed all that I can pray,
And I've said all that I can say,
When my heart can't take anymore,
My strength is depleted, and I feel defeated
This hurt I can't ignore

It's destroying me inside,
I can no longer hide
Tired of being tired
Dear Lord, if you are listening

Wash me, Oh Lord, make me whole again
Only you can console this pain and remove every stain
That there will be life again
Savior, don't pass me by
I've cried and I'm still crying to you
I feel lost and confused
Dear Lord, please Lord, come to my rescue

When I've thought it over a thousand times,
When I've done all that I know how,
My mind is going round and round
So many hopes fill my head, but I end up empty instead
Trying to look up but going down
It's destroying me inside,
I can no longer hide
Tired of being tired
Dear Lord, can you hear me?

I need to be washed, Oh Lord,
make me whole again
Only you can console this pain
and remove every stain
That there will be life again
Savior, please don't pass me by,
I've cried and I'm still crying to you
I feel lost and confused
Dear Lord, please Lord, come to my rescue

And God says...

I'm here
I've always been right here

I'll strengthen you to carry you through
I am your rescue, here to protect you
I'll give you what you need
Come find rest, you can rest in me

There are some mountains to be moved,
some created by what we say
There are some roads
you will never have to travel
Others you chose and they led you astray
In the midst of whatever may come,
I remain constant from day to day
Dear Child, I hear you
I have been speaking
Listen for me along the way

Scriptures to minister to your thoughts:

Psalm 34   **John 16:13-14**

UNITY

U-N-I-T-Y
Say it loud, U-N-I-T-Y
There is a unity
that should be in our communities,
not just on paper for us to read
Or just in our minds to hope or believe
BUT a reality

That is tangible beyond today
One Lord, One Faith
One Baptism, no schisms or isms in the Body of Christ
For we came to unite, on one accord
Understanding that in times like these…
WE NEED A SAVIOR, everyone is shouting
blessed and highly favored,
But we strive not just to be blessed,
but to become the blessing
No time to be messing around
With those who are content in procrastination
No destination
Knowing but refusing to do
Doing without the knowledge necessary
To address the adversary
And you wonder why the question is asked,
who are you?
Not amongst men, but in the Kingdom realm,
Are we embracing our identity or are we embracing
enmity against our God our Creator?
Or as Grandma says, Our mind regulator
Who woke us up early this morning,
and started us on our way
But He does not just wake us up out of a physical sleep
He wakes us up to life, and life more abundantly
Because we believe, we see
Signs, miracles, and wonders
Our praise, sounding like thunder
Our love, electrifying like the lightning
Our worship, thick and rising like the clouds
And some may wonder how?
It's a SUPERNATURAL thing

Growth, Change, and Development
No time for settlement
Because WE DO FAITH
Serving a God who has never lost a case
Full **A**ssurance **I**n **T**he **H**oly Ghost
So to those who were wondering,
You should now know…
When supernatural people
Come together with one accord,
Supernatural things are bound to happen
Because we serve a Naturally Super God

(In dedication to great Patriarchs Apostle PO Coleman along with all of the Supernatural family and Apostle David A.A. Mungo, Pastor Brenda Mungo along with the family of Guiding Light)

Scriptures to minister to your thoughts:

Psalm 133   **1 Corinthians 12:12-31**

Philippians 2:2-3

I wrote this poem for a Fifth Sunday Fellowship with Apostle PO "Only One" Coleman. Thank you for the FAITH acronym. You are a blessing in my life, and I appreciate you greatly.

Much Love Always!!!

My Senses

(Dedicated to my Dad, James "Cookie" Brooks Jr.)
I hear...
The words never spoken
The songs never sung
The melodies never played

I see...
The tears never cried
The hurt never told
The pain covered up inside

I feel...
The lashes of silent anger
The bruises of the past
The wounds of the present

I smell...
The fear of fear
The stench of hatred
The sourness of the unlearned

But I taste and see that the Lord is good
Blessed is the man that trusteth in Him

There is yet HOPE

Scriptures to minister to your thoughts:

Romans 4:16-18   **1 Peter 1:3-5**

Blindspot

You are looking at a road,
a path you are traveling
that's continually unraveling
bits and pieces of who you are
You are so close and yet so far
apart from the YOU that you should be
And the You
that's constantly assessing
your progress
Always less, always stressing
Over the next phase of the journey,
Yet in the midst of the doubt ever learning,
But not always applying the knowledge
to the situations of life
You are looking, you are seeking
Don't disregard your sight
as God is continually revealing
bits and pieces of who you are
Keep Him close and you will go far

Scriptures to minister to your thoughts:

Matthew 6:33-34   **Philippians 4:6**

Luke 12:25-31

Part 3

Think On His STRENGTH

The Name of the Lord is a STRONG tower: the righteous runneth into it, and is safe. (Proverbs 18:10)

Fight On

All of my problems staring me in the face
I'm being surrounded by spirits of despair and
hopelessness, and they're moving in fast

I'm trying to cope,
trying to keep up my head
But instead,
It's as if I am drowning in misery
And I'm asking, "How did this come to be?"

But wait a minute

I see you, yes Satan, I recognize you
And you have no control; my soul, it belongs to the Lord
I see you looking and you're thinking that I'm sinking
But I will rise in victory
You can't kill the FIGHT in ME

The pressure is compiling and not letting up
I'm praying, I'm serving
but all my problems are still there,
Going nowhere
I tried talking to friends
for an encouraging word,
But it seems absurd
My problems keep staring back at me

But it's just a trick of the enemy

So yes Satan, I see you and I recognize you

You have no control, I belong to the Most High,
I belong to the Lord
I see you looking and you're thinking that I'm sinking
But I will rise in VICTORY
You can't kill the FIGHT in ME

I have to shake the devil off
The struggle is real,
Lord, how many times do I go against your will?
ENOUGH!
I won't even, though I could
because I know all things work together for my good
And I don't even, though some say I should
because if I would
In HELL would I lift up my eyes - We're wasting time,
Complaining about battles warring against you and me
Because if Satan wins?
We'll be warring with fire for eternity

See, we as soldiers have to stand
and having done all to stand,
Continue to wave the blood-stained banner in our hands

NO – Not in defeat, we wave in VICTORY
Over poverty, over sickness, over death, over pain,
Over jealousy, over sin, over the things that "they said"
Yeah, we FIGHT on, we PRESS on
WE LIVE ON

Because the death that Satan desires for you and me
God granted us an exemption

when Jesus died on Calvary

Now yes, at times you get frustrated, it gets
complicated, you're no longer elated
Over the things that God said
that He would do
Because from the outside looking in,
you don't see them happening for you
And it's easier to quit, to give in, to give up
You're tired of being tired and enough is enough

BUT – What if Jesus had done the same
Instead, He tells us to call on His name
That's what the Holy Spirit calls us to do
To call Him, to pray, even when we don't want to
When you're born again, there is a fervor
that will not die
It pulls when you push,
it tugs when you don't even want to try

Ok soldiers, time to get in formation to tell the nations
That YES, this is the day
that the Lord has made
And in good or bad, I'll bless His name
Don't get me wrong, we fall down
But with wings of an eagle, we are raised
Having been blazed through the fire,
Watch us come out, out like pure gold
With testimonies to be told
Whether the call is for you to go,
Whether the call is to be still and know,
His plan, His command

His voice, But He gave us a choice
To keep on fighting on the battlefield of life
To all my true soldiers,
Let's fight the GOOD FIGHT

Scriptures to minister to your thoughts:

2 Timothy 2:3-4   **Ephesians 6:10-17**

This is the first spoken word I ministered at Grace Tabernacle Holiness Church with some great men and women of God. It was a pleasure and a blessing.

I dedicate this poem to the Cochrell and Miracle families, who carry a zeal for inspiring the Body of Christ.

Thank you for your testimonies!

A New Beginning

God, I can't see it, God, I can't feel it
God, I don't understand
My mind can't seem to comprehend

Between your Word and what I see
Between your promises and my reality,
I'm hoping greater for my latter
if I can make it through this battle

Lord if it were up to me,
I'd leave it all behind
I don't want to stay in this place
Don't know how much longer I can fight
But Lord, the spirit is willing
I've got to give it another try
Just as you spoke the world into existence

Speak now Lord, let your Word be my beginning

Scriptures to minister to your thoughts:

Philippians 3:13-14   **Romans 8:35-39**

Don't Break Before the
Breaking Point

Stretched beyond perceived capabilities,
Pulled in opposite directions,
Rejections of its abilities
To do more, To be more
Not just for games of tug-a-war

Strands are beginning to weaken and break
Some points together yet apart, the start
Of intensified pressure, more weight

It's the final moment
and you feel you can't hold on
Your feet are slipping,
You've been fighting so long

You feel the urge to let go
but why accept defeat?
It's when you hold fast
that you obtain victory
The pull is to progress you farther
than where you've been
For even if you fall,
you can get back up again

The moment of truth
There is a sudden release
Broken, Unraveled
The pulling has ceased
And you see

You made it

Scriptures to minister to your thoughts:

Galatians 6:9   **Isaiah 40:29-31**

Women With Purpose

(Dedicated to Chenise "MzChozen" Williams, founder of KBO, and all the beautiful women of WWP)

We are not here just to be here
We do not just exist, we choose to be alive
Each day we awake it's for a reason
And we choose not to compromise
We are women with purpose

Strong and beautiful, gifted and skilled
Talented and smart,
And still in the Master's will
We are women with purpose

Our light, it shines for all to see
Our bodies are covered as they should be
The Word, we study fearfully
We are women with purpose

Scriptures to minister to your thoughts:

Proverbs 31:10-31

Super Woman

Superwoman, Superwoman
How mighty you are
You are a beacon of light shining amongst the stars
Beauty and brains
Are one in the same
Humble, meek, and strong enough to reign
And reign you must, to get it all done
Whether by the moon's light
or rays of the sun
But tell me Superwoman,
who grants thee rest?
When work is incomplete,
Yet you've given your best
Your strength is strained with a load
others can't carry themselves
You continue to pour out, being left with empty shelves
And that you do receive
is poured out for immediate use
With your cupboard left empty,
for much you are required to do

Superwoman when do you stop?
To refill? To replenish?
Do you continue to heal others' wounds
but leave yourself with blemish?
How long will you continue
to procrastinate in the haste of life?
Declaring it to be ministry,
family, and sacrifice
Superwoman, Superwoman

Please hear as you continue to stand
When God called you for His purpose,
He did not leave you out of His plan.

Scriptures to minister to your thoughts:

Luke 10:38-42   **Matthew 11:28-30**

Part 4

Think On The BEAUTY OF HIS LOVE

Love never fails…

(1 Corinthians 13: 8).

What I can now say that I love about love is that it will persevere through the toughest of times while still yet knowing how to BE tough at times. Even when anger comes or perhaps temptations arise, LOVE conquers all. It should be our ultimate truth and responsibility to those that God has allowed to be in our lives.

Love Again

I almost thought that love was over
Almost thought that this was it
Thought I'd never find that special someone
You know, like that shoe with the perfect fit
The one you can go anywhere with

Not just because they're comfortable
Or fond to your eyes
Not just because they're stunning
And took your breath by surprise

But more so, you are given an assurance
You are secured just right
Every curve, every pressure point supported
Not too loose, not too tight

Now I know a love with new beginnings
Every day, a new spark is lit
I've found my special someone
Just like that shoe with the perfect fit

Scriptures to minister to your thoughts:

Ecclesiastes 4:9-12   **Jeremiah 29:11**
Ezekiel 16:8   **Romans 12:9**

Forever My King

Your very presence speaks a magnitude of volume
Yet you speak no words

Howbeit, when you do speak, your words can tame the roaring lion
While in the same instance handle the most fragile glass

You are the epitome
of what every man should strive to be

You are the essence of love, strength, grace,
and honor manifested in the natural

You are the flame that lights my candle, melts my heart,
and burns in my soul

Forever My King

Scriptures to minister to your thoughts:

Song of Solomon 2; 8:6-7   1 Peter 3:1-7

Ode of Love

(Tribute for my sister's wedding)

The way that I feel,
with words is hard to describe

Yes, we have our moments
but what I feel is real inside
Through all the ups and downs and tears
that we have cried
I'm grateful the Lord has brought us through somehow

Because I love being in love with you
Nobody else will do
I make this vow for life
Just take my hand, and we'll go through
Whatever we have to do
Our lives are just beginning and I'm willing
To share my life's journey with you

Scriptures to minister to your thoughts:

Genesis 2:18, 23-25   **I Corinthians 16:14**
Proverbs 18:22   **Mark 10:6-9**

A Wedding Song

We've been through, oh so much
But we made it here today
Ups and downs, round and round
But we made it here today

And through it all, I can say
That I love you, yes I do
From start until the end
On me, you can depend
I will be there, thick or thin
Every part of me, wholeheartedly
In love with you

I may not get it right
the first time every time
There will be some rain,
but let's cherish the sunshine
If we let God be our guide,
we'll always make it through somehow

I give my heart this day
with you, I will always stay

Because I love you, yes I do
From start until the end
On me, you can depend
I will be there, thick or thin
Every part of me, wholeheartedly
In love with you

Scriptures to minister to your thoughts:

1 Corinthians 7:3-5, 10-17   Ephesians 5:21-32

I wrote and sang this song at my first wedding. Yes, I said first wedding (lol). Our marriage did not last, but the values gained helped me to become the wife I am today. I am grateful for my journey.

What a Man

(Tribute to Apostle Michael L. Richburg)

What a man, what a man, what a man,
what a mighty great man!
God fearing, with an endearing personality
To all that he meets
Kingdom walking, faith talking
Demon fighter, Holy Spirit igniter
This man, he teaches kingdom
The sheep, he feeds them
The people, he leads them

Into a greater destiny
A place they didn't think they could be
Because he sees beyond what they see,
walking in the five-fold ministry
Wisdom and knowledge
Revelator of the Word
This man is none other
Than Michael Richburg
What?! You haven't heard? Really?

Well let me be the first to say to you
Ever pressing and opening our eyes to the TRUTH
He'll make it do what it do, as he do what it does, Simply because…
He's anointed, he's appointed, and a true
Prophet of God--Then again,
Maybe you just don't wanna know
But you can't deny
The greater power that is working on the inside
Followed by signs, and wonders as a witness
Listen up, you need to get this
If he tells you the berries are ripe,
Then go get your bucket
Gottalmighty,
Got to tell you I'm lovin' it
He'll make you feel it, taste it, see it, & touch it
By the time it's all over, you'll be like, "What…
Is it, that has happened to me?"
I'll tell you what happened
Potential just met destiny
That you will be able to tell the world
That Jesus lives, being able to give
Becoming a resource of the source,

And staying the course,
Adhering to the foundation that has been laid
Somebody ought to clap your hands
and give Jesus a praise

And keep on clapping for 43 years of ministry
Push your neighbor and tell them
I hear the sound of victory
Because above all else,
he has been faithful to the call
Ups and downs along the way,
but he shall recover ALL
We may not be able to give
all that you deserve,
But honor is surely due to a great leader
Apostle Michael L. Richburg

Scriptures to minister to your thoughts:

1 Timothy 5:17-18

*This poem was written at the celebratory services of the man
that I am blessed to have as my husband and leader.*

Mother's May I?

*(Tribute to my mother Carolyn Levine, my grandmother Ollie Mae
Dinkins, all the Great Women in my family, the Beautiful Seasoned
Citizens of Sumter Senior Services, and to Mothers everywhere)*

Mothers, may I tell you
how great you really are?
Your example made your children reach for the stars
And even farther,
Because you worked harder
That they would not have to
go through all the things that you have been through

Mothers, may I tell you
the depth of your greatness?
There is not a factory that could make this
genuineness that makes you, you!
That can do all that you do
And then some, good and bad
May have lost along the way,
but thank God for what you had

Mothers, may I tell you
the force that you are in the earth?
From you doctors, lawyers, and presidents are birthed
And that is merely the beginning
You keep sending the truth in love,
And that's a constant
that we all are in need of

Mothers, may I tell you

even if you don't hear it anymore,
You are loved and appreciated
For YOU we thank God for

Mothers, may I tell you
even if you don't see it with your own eyes,
You are on stage with a crowded room applauding
Stand up and take your bow

Mothers, may I tell you
even if you never smell the roses you deserve,
There is a field of plenty, every flower you can name
That is testifying of your worth
Mothers, may I tell you
even if you never taste
the restaurants' finest cuisine,
To a child, nothing beats Mama's kitchen
We'll pull up a chair any day of the week

Mothers, may I tell you
even if you never feel
the return of the love you give,
Smile and be thankful
you have the love to share
And blessed to be a mother with life to live

Mothers, I MUST tell you
Your presence is a light shining bright as the sun
Today and every day, thank you,
Thank you for a job well done
Happy Mother's Day

Scriptures to minister to your thoughts:

Ephesians 6:1-3   **Proverbs 31:10, 28-31**

I have truly been blessed with great Aunts who have been purposeful in my life and my children's. Thank you for all your love, sacrifice, and care! Much love always!

PART 5

Think On His WORSHIP

Worship is not confined to a moment of experiencing the presence of God's glory. It is not limited to the lyrics and beautiful sounds of music that invoke the fruit of our lips to flow with reverence unto our God. Worship honors God with our lives, our whole being.

Release

We release the sound of Worship
We release the sound of Praise
We release the sound,
Fall fresh upon us now
We release the Sound

Scriptures to minister to your thoughts:

Psalm 34:1-3

Sometimes the simplest words can minister a profound revelation to our spirit.

WORSHIP SONG

I want my worship to be pure before you Father,
In Spirit and in truth
Not simply for material manifestations
Not just because of things that you do,
But because of WHO you are
None compares to your love
None compares to your presence
And Glory from above
My heart sings your worship

And my lips give the fruit thereof
Inhabit my praise Father
Smell the sweet savor of my worship
Flow in the melodies
not conformed to this earthly realm
Treasures in this vessel shining forth the power of your true self

Scriptures to minister to your thoughts:

Psalm 93   **John 4:23-34**

The Glory in the Story

You see the glory,
but you don't know the story
Behind the person you see
Tragedies and victories
The battle wounds that have mended and
some of which are still healing, BUT
I am still yet believing God

You see the glory,
but you don't know the story
Of the road that I have traveled,
Walking towards a future with a past unraveled in my present, BUT
I am forgiven and presented faultless
before the presence of HIS glory

You see the glory, but you don't know the story
of the mess God delivered me from
How far I have come
Falling down and getting up
Some traps set by the enemy and some
from my own crazy stuff, BUT
HIS love covers a multitude of sin

You see the glory,
making an assumption by my smile
By my clothes, by my shoes, but if in my
shoes, you could walk a mile
You would understand my story
You would understand my praise
You would understand my worship and why I glorify His name

The glory you see is not so much of me
It all belongs to God
My life tells of His story
How He will cover
and lift you when you fall
How He will answer when you call
How He chastises and brings correction
while loving you through it all
How while we were still yet in sin,
His grace and mercy did abound
And still, yet we are not worthy, BUT
He chooses us anyhow
To be the head and not the tail
To be above and not beneath
To be a light that cannot be hidden
Soaring like eagles, WE ARE HIS MOUTHPIECE

And we are all called as part of the kingdom
Not for a soliloquy
That His glory will be all of our Story
Many members of one body

Scriptures to minister to your thoughts:

Psalm 34:1   **Romans 8**

*(This poem can be added on to if to be done for
tribute, add-on originally done for tribute to Bishop
Calvin J. Sanders, my cousin. I love you.)*

And today we give honor to a laborer worthy of his hire

The fullness of his story yet to be told,
how he's been tried in the fire

Not for spectators to watch and see
Or dictators to dictate how his life should be
Nor for manipulators to control
the outcome of destiny
Or speculators to form an opinion from their
blinded observation, be it truthful or falsely
For it is not your story
and it is not for your glory

Scriptures to minister to your thoughts:

2 Corinthians 1:3-5

Pure

With a clear conscience and hopeful heart,
I pursue your glory to be fulfilled in me
On a joyful journey, I triumphantly travel,
humbled in your presence to be
I come with everything I have,
knowing that all I have is yours
Trusting that the Holy Spirit
will lead and guide me to the right doors
Your Word I pray, with Faith I pursue
Not sure of my direction,
Nevertheless, my assurance is in you

My heart yearns to be pleasing
and righteous in your sight
Though I find joy in life's simple pleasures,
It is in your Word that I delight
When I am in your presence, oh what peace is mine
Your promises are fulfilled
when I stay connected to the vine
I have fallen, I have stumbled,
while seeking the righteous way
I have felt lost on this journey,
Yet my heart desires not to stray
In man's eyes, I am blemished
In man's eyes, I am flawed
In man's eyes, my path is predicted by my past
with no potential of my call
Let my eyes view your heart in me
Let my eyes see what you see
Your Word is a lamp unto my feet
Holy Spirit, you are my purity
Lead me to captivity
Chained to a love I cannot break free
Locked by the bars of liberty
Uniformed by clothing of grace and mercy
For I have been charged, I am sentenced to life
My body is presented a living sacrifice

Scriptures to minister to your thoughts:

Leviticus 8:35   **2 Timothy 3:14-17**

Romans 12:1-3

PART 6

Think On His TRUTH

"I am the Way, and the Truth, and the Life"…(John 14:6). We spend much time trying to convince others of a truth we ourselves are not certain of. We get caught up in the Facts of Life instead of focusing on the Promises of His Truth. We have a source who is sure. Let us trust in Him and not lean to our own understanding (Proverbs 3:5).

Uncertainty

In the beginning, there is much assurance
You have endurance
To run effortlessly, endlessly
Consistently going without thinking about
the obstacles that may lie ahead
Confidently, naively
Dismissing sorrowful tears to be shed
You only see the Son
So bright, so much light
Shines through to your nights,
Overcoming any darkness that seeks to consume
Happiness and joy overtake any gloom
As days turn to weeks,
months, and then years
The confidence that you had
doesn't seem so near
You get tired, your desires
Aspire to get to that place where you now only visit
And these things
were always there for the ride
Over time, we look behind only to find
Instead of properly being handled, we tossed them aside

The path that once was clear
is now cluttered
Now that we must cross the way again,
our mind becomes fluttered
Discouragement, loss of hope
Unable to cope
With things around and thoughts within

And in this moment of uncertainty,
confusion begins

You're not sure what to think, what to do, where to go
Whether or not you're in the right direction,
and if so, how do you know?

Do you keep moving forward,
doing the best you can?
Do you trace your steps backwards,
hoping to reveal a plan?
Do you remain still, not moving at all?
Do you shout for help?
Who would answer your call?
Why do we allow uncertainty to create doubt about the
unchanging, everlasting, omnipotent God we serve?

He is constant
In the midst of our wavering sea
He is the voice that calls us to walk into a
place in Him that brings peace
in the midst of the storm
So when the holes of uncertainty come
to create a void, we fill it with
the Word which makes us whole in Him.

Scriptures to minister to your thoughts:

James 1:5-8

Religion

Just like gold-plated jewelry--We bask in
the glory of the layer outside,
but there comes a time
When
The old that was harbored within
will taint what was new and you
find yourself fighting to hold on to the residue
Of a virtual emotion that has
shunned you from the reality of truth
Your eyes wide shut,
Your ears openly deaf
A numbing sensation that continues until you have nothing left,
which has now become your rite of passage
to a door that was
ALWAYS open to you

All you had to do is ask
All you had to do is seek
All you had to do is knock
Instead, we have locked Him out of
His own temple

We have conformed to the religiosity of an inspired
moment opposed to the irrepressible freedom in
His presence
How can He have His way if we are always in the way?
This day, choose whom ye will serve
And let the Word
be your eyes to wisdom and understanding as the
Holy Spirit leads and guides you into all truth

The door was always open
What happens next is up to you

Scriptures to minister to your thoughts:

Matthew 7:7-8   **Colossians 2:6-10**

Value

Value
Is it to be counted as according to monetary worth?
Being added and subtracted,
adjacent to the ups and downs of life
Placed at a standard price -
Possibility to be stolen, Potentiality to be counterfeited,
But never admitted
Confiscating the real truth
In hopes of concealing the value in you

Value
Is it to be measured
as liquid pouring into a pitcher or glass?
Predestinating the outcome
Being poured into or taken from
Never to exceed the measurement given
Manipulated control
You may think but you will never see
You're just a listed ingredient
in a fated recipe

Forced into a blended truth,
The only value seen
is a mixture of others' view

Value
A simulation to our purpose in the kingdom
Not to be counted, not to be measured, but treasured
Our value becomes infinite, limitless
as we optimally contend
To grow in knowledge of Him,
Our Father, neglecting the world's sinful end
A Believer's value leads to **V**ictory
A Believer's value allows you to **A**chieve
A Believer's value gives **L**ife and **L**ove
Understanding and is **E**difying
Its totality is not conclusive in words or people
You can search but the fullness is not in them
There is only One who is invaluable,
And our true value lies in HIM.

Scriptures to minister to your thoughts:

2 Corinthians 4:6-7   **1 Corinthians 15:10**

Vulnerable

I am vulnerable here
I am just good at covering what's underneath
You say, "How you doing?"

I say, "I'm alright"
When really, I just don't want you to see

That I am vulnerable here
I am just good at making a disguise
What you see is all that you will get
My true feelings are internalized

Because I am vulnerable here
I have just learned how to mask the pain
Laugh to keep from crying
My spirit dying,
Having to lose and not able to gain

So, you are vulnerable here
Is "here" your expected end?
To acknowledge what is
Is not a settlement of where you are
Healing is yours; decide when it will begin

So, you are vulnerable here
Is vulnerability your excuse
To become comfortable with a form
That continually does you harm,
Having potential that will never be of use?

So, you are vulnerable here
Is your shame greater than your pain?
Choosing to remain covered,
Because of the opinions of others,
All for the sake of saving your name

What is vulnerability but an inoperability
with lack of consistency
towards the potential that could be
free from circling endlessly
exposing the "inner me"
that hinders your true ability
stagnated by a one-sided reality
that focuses on the negativity
drawing from the plurality
of problems, pain, and ignorancy,
while rejecting the hope of expectancy
in the true Living God who supplies
ALL needs
It is His Kingdom and righteousness I seek
He helps my unbelief,
knows what I cannot see
His grace is sufficient,
and His power perfect when I'm weak

Scriptures to minister to your thoughts:

2 Corinthians 12:9-10   **1 Peter 2:15-21**

HURT

I'm hurt and I know it,
yet reluctant to let my heart show it.
Encased by fear, from the words I hear
when it's my own lips that have sown it.

I'm hurt and I feel it,
yet too proud in my heart to reveal it.
To softly cry or bottle up inside,
I will be the only one to see it.

I'm hurt and I hold it,
becoming my truth as I mold it.
I blindly see, and let things be, that which is
won't be because I told it.

I'm hurt and I can control it,
letting go without letting go of it.
I block any shame,
and any reaction that came,
while the heart protects any hole in it.
I'm hurt and I release it,
to do anything else leaves me in pieces.
To be whole with holes
and completely incomplete,
smiling with a frown,
trying to heal my mind while my heart bleeds.

But if I let go, I may hurt—this I know.
The hurt that I feel that once held me here,
the hurt that was tamed
is no longer to blame
for my forfeit of liberty
TODAY BE MADE FREE!!! I AM.......

Scriptures to minister to your thoughts:

Galatians 5:1, 7-8

PART 7

Think On His Joy

To have joy goes beyond a state of being happy. I have heard it preached many times that happiness comes from happenings, but JOY comes from the Lord!

Isn't that just like our God to bring the beauty out of something that might otherwise be overshadowed by gloom? Sing! Shout! Leap! Let your JOY be complete in Him!

Count It All Joy

I count it all joy
My heartache and pain
My storms, my rain
It won't take me out, it's ok
I count it all joy
Because it's not my ending
I'm just being shaped
Into a brand new me—just wait and see
When I reap my blessings

So many things try to press me down,
Turn my smile into a frown,
Try to stress me
Don't want me to reap my blessings
Trouble comes, but it won't last always
And it won't determine the depth of my PRAISE!
Satan comes to steal, kill, and destroy
But the Word says to count it all joy
So, I count it all joy
My heartache and pain
My storms, my rain
It won't take me out, it's ok
I count it all joy
Because it's not my ending
I'm just being shaped
Into a brand new me—just wait and see
When I reap my blessings

Clouds form, winds blow, storms come,
But the sun is still shining

and I am delighted in Him!

Scriptures to minister to your thoughts:

James 1:2-4   **Psalm 34:1-3**

Light Up the City

This girl is fire! Yes, with a flame so bright that it cannot be hidden
In the darkest night, in the brightest day
Shine so that all men may see
Not you, not me
But the Father in Heaven,
Glorifying Him continually
My brethren, my sisters,
Blessing Him at all times
And when negative things come to mind,
You have to block it, stop it, cut it
Because what it does is it covers our light
And instead of shining, we're blinding people from the Great God
that we say we serve
And we get trapped in the place of "I heard"
When we should know Our Father firsthand
but we no longer know Him
The One who thought we were worth saving!
Who we have Faith in
And we then begin to live in testimonies of our past
But we say we serve Him every day
Are we truly shining our light

so that others can find the way?
Or are we too busy liking what we see when we're
looking at the "me" that's in the mirror,
missing the clearer picture
that the Father wants us to see?

Let's light up the city
Let's get in a haste
No time to waste
Let us taste and see how good He is
Walk and do those things that are like He is
For He is the way, the truth, and the light
He increases my strength
when I have no might
My plight is to fulfill His purpose
To Be a Living Sacrifice is
My reasonable service

Scriptures to minister to your thoughts:

Matthew 5:14-16   **John 8:12**

Song of Victory

Hard times stress my mind
Try to take me out
But greater is He that lives in me
You see, I been there
Through depression, rejection

But oh for His grace
And mercy

I'm so thankful, so grateful for
ALL God has done
My victory is won

They slayed me
Felt like I was crucified
But the price has been paid
I'm under His blood
So I won't think it strange
When trials come, and they will
For my God, He reigns
And I reign with Him

I'm so thankful, so grateful for
ALL God has done
My victory is won

Scriptures to minister to your thoughts:

2 Timothy 2:12   **2 Corinthians 2:14**

1 Peter 2:13-14

Perspective

Do you see the flowers of the field?

By itself? All alone?

I see strength and endurance

and the beauty that is shown

Do you see the tree with leaves?

Drying up and dying?

I see foundation

and the season of God's perfect timing

Do you see the sun?

Scorching hot and blinding light?

I see the warmth of the Father

showing His delight

Do you see the mountains of snow and ice?

Freezing temperatures? Bringing cold?

I see a blanket of righteousness

that comes to console

Do you see the destruction of the wind?

Rampaging the land?

I see new beginnings with a helping hand

Do you see the flooding of the rain?

Constantly pouring all around?

I see the Holy Spirit moving

with peaceful sounds

Do you see the lightning and thunder?

Flashes and booms? Piercing the sky?
I see an illuminated wonder
and music from on High

Do you see the bugs, the birds, the bears?
Creatures of all sorts?
I see the beauty of God's creation
and His purposeful art
What is your perspective?

Scriptures to minister to your thoughts:

Psalm 104:24-34   **Romans 1:20**

I dedicate this poem to my Dad Claude Levine. He has encouraged me and pushed me towards my goals, always challenging me to have eyes from every angle. Thank you.

PART 8

Thoughts
To
THINK
ABOUT

Matters of the Heart

Love and hate
Intermingle in the same space
What we hear or what we feel,
Or is it what we see
that determines what's real?

Joy and sadness
Bittersweet moments of gladness
Make haste or meditate?
What determines the amount of time we contemplate?

The tortoise or the hare?
Or do we even care?
To move quick or to move slow?
What is it that determines our ability to go?

Steadfast but with hesitation
Sure? Unsure?
Ups and downs of communication,
Bold and shy
With whom, for what, where, when, why
Nonchalant and expectation,
Wavering between a torn sensation

Confident and apprehensive?
What determines if we are
assertive or defensive?
Not enough and too much
Somewhere in the middle feeling stuck

Wealth and prosperity
Taking dives into poverty
Dreams and realities
What factors determine the extent of our possibilities?

So many Matters of the Heart

Scriptures to minister to your thoughts:

Romans 8:35-39

Relationships

Is it a choice or an obligation?
Done because of love or because of stipulations
That may or may not affect
that which you want to obtain?
Is it my will you seek?
Or my heart you desire to gain?
Fear created,
bringing condemnation to the mind,
bondage to the soul, to stagnation you become tied
Not sure if you are going forth
or moving at all
You heard, YES YOU HEARD
But fear decided not to answer the call

Perfect love casts out fear,
But what develops when love becomes conditional?

Submissive to the heights and pitfalls of an emotional roller coaster,
Love is good, but not producing to receive
You give and you take
while still yet not fulfilling your needs
When does loyalty become a requirement
and not a gift of the heart?
When does kindness become a duty
and not a desire on our part?
When does love become responsibility
and not the essence of who we are?

We will only get but so far
Until we reach the locked door with contention
Who is doing the locking,
and will that door ever grant permission?
It is not you, it is me,
Or is it not me, it is you?
We avoid the inevitable place
of facing ourselves in truth
How can we relate,
if we never communicate?
We already made up our mind
on when we will participate
How can we draw near if we never listen, and only hear,
Responding out of emotion
and perception of a picture that is unclear?

Scriptures to minister to your thoughts:

1 John 4

Two-Way Street

To the Women

I need a listening ear from all my single ladies
Stop laying up with these so-called men
and having their babies
Being labeled as their maybe
I will, Maybe I won't; Give you a call on the telephone
Making promises with lines you already heard
Wait a minute, let me finish
With this thing that produces no good,
I wish a Queen would
Be a Queen, who is strong,
even when you feel weak,
Knowing how and when to speak
You must not know 'bout me
Yes, a prize but not able to be won
This jewel can be found if you first find the Son

To the Men

Who are you? Not just another baby daddy
Being trapped by what you see
Because you thought that she would be the one
Brothers, stop letting the flesh blind you from the mess,
designed to impress the eyes
And make you compromise
your inheritance and your rights
To be the head and a King
Understand you need a Queen, not just any old thing
Royalty calls you higher
for the crown to lawfully be laid
So when you hear the howls,

See what is not shown, hear what is not said

Scriptures to minister to your thoughts:

1 Peter 3:1-7   **Colossians 3:18-19**

Servant

Hey! Look at me!
Yes, I am a servant in the kingdom

But don't catch me on the wrong day
I don't know what may come
out of my mouth
I may be feeling some type of way

Hey! Look at me!
Yes, I am a servant in the kingdom

But it depends on what you
may ask me to do
I cannot give all my money all the time
You see, I have my own desires too

Hey! Look at me!
Yes, I am a servant in the kingdom

But don't try to get me to do a lot of work
Let me know what it is; I might be available

I do enough already in the church

Hey! Look at me!
Yes, I am a servant in the kingdom
But as long as I can get something for me,
I am anointed and appointed; I know a lot
I am called for greatness, can't you see?
Hey! Servant!
Yes, you servant in the kingdom
Is that what you proclaim to be?
I thought a true servant does not do
what they want to
when and how they see

Hey! Servant!
Yes, you servant in the kingdom
Is that who you boast to be?
Yet every other day you complain
And you act as if it is a strain
To do things necessary for ministry

Hey! Servant!
Yes, you servant in the kingdom
Is that what you pridefully say?
You are trying to lead
And not effectively follow
And when you do follow,
it's not in the right way

Hey! Servant!
Yes, you servant in the kingdom
So you're the anointed one, the called?

Tell me, who are you called to?
Yourself? Your flesh?
You give in part, but justify it to be all

Scriptures to minister to your thoughts:

Mark 10:42-45   **John 12:26**

Untitled

You say I did? I say I didn't.
The truth of the matter?
Who's willing to admit it?
Whether it makes you right,
whether it makes you wrong,
The TRUTH is the TRUTH, all day long

Our eyes have become slanted
We have paused the DVD,
Gazing at one moment in a picture
Instead of watching the full movie in HD

You see a sofa, I see a couch
To me, it doesn't matter
But for you, it must be figured out

Let's try something different
With no goal to prove or to compete
If we stand back to view the objective,

We'll see there is space for more than one seat
We can agree to disagree, respectfully apart
Without carrying any malice
or grudges a la carte
So what if I did? So what if you didn't?
The truth of the matter?
We both should be willing to admit it

Taking responsibility for our actions,
Being conscious of our words,
Slow to speak and swift to hear
That the truth may be heard

Scriptures to minister to your thoughts:

Matthew 5:23-24   **Proverbs 18:2, 12-21**

Presumed Not Innocent

I hear you pre-playing my words in your mind
as we converse in the solitude of your thoughts,
based on assumptions of what I ought—
Or not ought to say
For you knew me in my yesterday
and what is it that you are presumed to know?
As you speak from a past future
whose emotion only you continue to grow
For even when I speak with or without words

Your voice is the only voice that you have heard
Do you continue to listen with a closed ear?
Trying by a Spirit with motives unclear
It is the Holy Spirit that leads and guides into all Truth
What would be the outcome
with evidence presented for you?

Scriptures to minister to your thoughts:

Matthew 7:1-5   **Leviticus 19:15-16**

John 7:24   **1 John 4:13**

Words We Speak

I hear you say what you can't do, what you
don't have, what you can't see
From the same fountain, you flow Biblical words,
Who is the God in your heart of which you speak?
Or have you rehearsed religious quotes
to create a tune pleasant to the ear,
creating a good sound,
but delivering a message that is unclear?
Who hears words of contention,
yet justify all to be truth?
If we are to cast down imaginations,
what images are you keeping in your view
to make your first response always a question
or self-centered promotion?

If holiness is to be your lifestyle,
how can you serve in part-time devotion?
With a notion to lawfully strive,
with a notion to do good,
proclaiming a hope of what you could've done,
what you would've done, or that others should
So we go through changes with no growth,
Seeing a difference while we ourselves never become
the difference we desire to be
Being spiritual, but not able to spiritually see
Who then has accountability if we choose to disregard?
Who is responsible if we choose to receive in part,
And choosing which part
that we will or will not receive?
Do we only yearn for our desires
and neglect what we really need?

Scriptures to minister to your thoughts:

James 3:11-12   **Psalm 37:4-5**
1 Corinthians 12:31   **James 1:8**

PART 9

Think On His COMFORT

Sorrow and grief are a part of life. At times, it may seem unbearable to our hearts and minds. This is when His joy is our strength. Strength to smile, strength to make it through the day, and strength for whatever you need. This is a day the Lord has made for you to be glad and rejoice in it. You may be weeping, but pause for a moment to see what the day holds through God's eyes. You are special to Him, and He did not leave you comfortless. Do not allow life's pressures to cause you to fear or hesitate to grasp His promises, even if you do not yet fully understand.

LaToya Richburg

Ode to My Grandmother

This poem is dedicated to my Great Grandmother Evelena Dennis

The only reference to great is to your character
Unconditional love like no other
The life you lived is an example for all
The reflection of a true Grandmother

I remember the days
I would sit at your feet of wisdom,
Listening to stories of things back then
You would throw in some smiles and laughter,
always ended with a hug that strengthened

Strengthened my spirit,
a warmth that consoled
Your presence is a gift, and food for the soul
Though I didn't see the moment you left,
Didn't see you go
Never knew it would have been our last time
on this side
Not sure if I wanted to know
Yes, it hurts and Yes, I feel pain
At times can't stop tears
from rolling down my face
Yes, it gets heavy and emotions arise
Can't find words to explain
how I'm feeling on the inside

I treasure the gift you are
In friendship and in family

A gift God knew I needed:
the gift of memories

Knowing your desire is not for me
to be consumed by sorrowful tears
Nor depressed or oppressed
from you having to leave this world here

There are times I get so overwhelmed
Because I miss you so much
Thinking of the comfort
to have just one more touch
And in that very moment,
through the tears, I begin to smile
Being comforted by your words
and presence in my mind

My heart is filled with peace
More and more as each day goes by
I am grateful for our time spent
I am grateful for your life

And I remember He is faithful
I remember He is true
In spite of what I feel, and what I go through

In every moment God is faithful
My Father is always true
Just as you are faithful God, make me faithful to you

Scriptures to minister to your thoughts:

Romans 8:18, 28   **2 Timothy 1:5**

John 16:20-22   **1 Thessalonians 4:13-18**

He Careth

In this life, we all have problems
We all have tests and trials
that we must go through
At times the burdens,
the BURDENS, are so heavy
The load seems too much to bear, and you don't know what to do

Just put your trust in God, for He knows
Yes, and He cares
He sees just what you're going through
Don't give up, Don't give in
He careth much for you

On this journey,
sometimes the tears, they fall
The sleepless nights, they come
And you'll find yourself pacing the floor
Your mind is clouded
With worry, grief, and pain
Nothing seems to work out right
And you just can't take it anymore

Just put your TRUST in God for
He KNOWS
Yes, and He CARES
He SEES just what you're going through
Don't give up, Don't give in
HE CARETH MUCH FOR YOU

Scriptures to minister to your thoughts:

1 Peter 5:6-7   **1 Corinthians 1:5-7**

John 14:1   **2 Corinthians 1:3-7**

Psalm 19

Too Soon...

(Dedicated to my Uncle Van Conyers Sr.,
always your Toyota)

It hit like a ton of bricks
When I realized this was it
The tears rolled; my heart cried,
Knowing I had to say good-bye
With no clear reason why
Other than God saw fit to take you home
And even though I saw it was your time,
A part of me did not want you to go

Still yet my heart has joy
Memories that will fill the void
The Father called,
you walked through the door
The pain you had,
you did not have to feel anymore
One of the reasons I give God thanks for

More than our grief

The Father's comfort is
I trust His promises are sure
Even while in my heart, you are truly missed

Scriptures to minister to your thoughts:

Matthew 5:4   **Psalm 34:18**
Matthew 11:28-30   **Psalm 73:26**

Much love always to My Aunt Kim and her children

(my cousins) VJ, AJ, Danielle, and Ashley with whom my children and I spent many days from childhood to adulthood. Thank you for sharing your heart and home.

My Hope Has Wings

(Dedicated to Clara Dennis (Godmother) whom I affectionately call "Ma", and all who have ever had to face cancer future, past, and present; may your hope never leave you comfortless)

My hope has wings
that will elevate me from the ground
That causes me to soar and not to be bound

My hope has wings
that spread in preparation for the flight
That causes me to soar towards a greater light

My hope has wings
that are able to fly
That causes me to soar beyond the view of my eyes

My hope has wings
to carry me on the winds
That causes me to soar
even when I feel I have no strength

My Hope rises, My Hope soars,
Continually seeking and knocking on doors
of Belief, of Promise, of Patience, of Love
And when there seems to be no doors,
I continue seeking above

Looking to the hills from where my help comes from
Leaning not to my own understanding
With all my heart I will trust
Because my Hope has wings
strong enough to rise above it all
And I will continue to rise and answer Hope's call

Scriptures to minister to your thoughts:

Proverbs 3:5-6   **Isaiah 40:31**
1 Peter 5:10

PART 10

RANDOM THOUGHTS

The poems in the last section of this book are not specifically titled. Sometimes I have thoughts or groups of words that come across my mind. I simply write them down.

Random Thoughts #1

The biggest enemy is the inner me
Who desires to see, but cannot see
Trying to look naturally
When it is through the Spirit if first must be
For what is faith, but to walk physically, blindly
Towards the purpose of destiny
A hope of expectancy
To manifest what has not been seen
A revelation not yet believed
A mind not elevated to receive
What is already within awaiting discovery

Scriptures to minister to your thoughts:

Hebrews 11:1-3, 6

Random Thoughts #2

So you say you're tired of trying
Where does that leave us from here?
Do we leave words unspoken,
Hearing with a deaf ear?

So you say you're tired of trying
Where do we go from here?
Do we suppress every emotion?
Do we bottle up our tears?

So you say you're tired of trying
Do you stay or do you go?
And if you stay, are you just existing?
If you go, are you resisting?
Who or what is determining the last say-so?

Scriptures to minister to your thoughts:

Galatians 6:9   **1 Corinthians 13:4-7**

Random Thoughts #3

Tell me I am wrong and that's ok,
But do not make that all that you should say
If all you can see is the wrong in me
You have torn down
Without any mirror to see

Communication for so many
is a one-way street
One directional, with no U-turns,
and no stops along the way to meet

Ever busy, always moving,
never taking a moment to slow down
To hear, to listen, to take in every sound

To see if you should stop,

adjust to the left or to the right
Take a stroll to enjoy the scenery,
the amusement, the sights
We speed hurriedly by,
often without knowledge of what we passed
Moments missed, words unspoken,
Time lost just to become first and not last

Scriptures to minister to your thoughts:

James 1:19   **Colossians 3:6**

Random Thoughts #4

Why do we force God into a box?
His ways are not our ways,
His thoughts are not our thoughts,
And yet we think He ought
To heed our desires
To our plans, To our timing
Without denying
Because after all, He understands
We are only human
We all sin and fall short of His glory
I wonder if on the day of Judgement,
Would we still have the same story?

Scriptures to minister to your thoughts:

Romans 11:34-36   1 Corinthians 2:9-16

Random Thoughts #5

Do I speak the truth that makes me free,
But leads you into captivity?

Words whose value lies only in the mind,
Living a life with a heart of denial

Love spoken, but yet to be known
An abundance from the lips without any action shown

Justified from thoughts within
A grace portrayed yet still condemned

Scriptures to minister to your thoughts:

**Proverbs 18:19-20   1 Corinthians 8:9-13
Matthew 5:23-26**

Random Thoughts #6

Life is given and then given away
Time is cherished,
but it does not come to stay

Just as the stars disappear into light's day,
Our vapor of life soon also will fade
As memories come,
with joys and tears, we pay
Relying on God's strength to console along the way
Sometimes in a moment,
grief causes us to stray
Yet love guides us back through mercy and grace
In all we do, In all we say
We shall give thanks, We shall give praise

Scriptures to minister to your thoughts:

John 10:10-18

The last poem in this book is dedicated to my sisters. We all have unique talents and gifts which make us the brilliant women we are!

We didn't steal it!

We have a beautiful mother

(Carolyn Levine) who passed on her strength. I always said, "Together, we are a force to reckon with!" We have overcome a lot in this journey of life. I love each and every one of you.

Shante

Jessica

Tameka

Jamie

From LaToya, with love

Photo by our Mom: Carolyn Levine

Sisters

We have argued, we have fought
We don't always see eye to eye
We are strong in our opinions
And our reasons why

We have good days and bad days,
Along with everything in between
With the ups and downs of life,
taking paths seen and unseen

Our words at times are harsh
Good intentions we don't always keep
Nevertheless, if danger comes,
the heart will surely speak

And say…

We are sisters
Alike and different in our identity
Yes, we are sisters
Through trials of our uncertainties
Sisters beyond any words
and all that life imparts
God has blessed us with each other
We are sisters of the heart
Even with the busy times of life,
We make time to share moments together
Stored treasure of memories,
My sisters in my heart forever

About the Author

I am the second oldest of five girls to James Brooks Jr. and Carolyn (Claude) Levine. South Carolina has always been my home. I am blessed to be a wife to Apostle Dr. Michael L. Richburg as well as a mother to a beautiful daughter (Ahnystie) and handsome son (Jeremiah). I love God! I have been blessed to serve in ministry under the leadership of Bishop Marvin Hodge Sr. (Nation Full Gospel Church), which is my home church. Pastor Marie Sanders (Anointed Word) is another wonderful woman of God who has been very instrumental in my ministerial journey as well as Apostle Dr. Phillip "Only One" Coleman. These great men and women of God are foundational leaders in my life. It is a blessing to serve with my Sister Min. Chenise Williams CEO and founder of Kingdom Builders Organization; alongside Min. Melika Walker, our sister, and co-laborer. Many great men and women of God have been influential in my life—some of which are referenced throughout this book. I am appreciative of them all! I currently serve at Divine Guidance Ministries where the Senior Pastor is my husband, Dr. Michael L. Richburg. However I can find my hands to be of help in ministry, I strive to do. One of my favorite scriptures is 2 Corinthians 4:7, "But we have this treasure in earthen vessels, that the excellency of the power may be of God, and not of us." To my family, friends, and all who have planted a seed in the garden of my life; I want to say thank you! If your name is not personally mentioned, please know you are no less valued.

Much Love Always!